100 REASONS WHY YOU SHOULD BE A SOCIALIST

Authored By Nor Luap

You Shouldn't

You Shouldn't

You Shouldn't

You Shouldn't

You Shouldn't

You Shouldn't

You Shouldn't

You Shouldn't

You Shouldn't

You Shouldn't

You Shouldn't

You Shouldn't

You Shouldn't

You Shouldn't

You Shouldn't

You Shouldn't

You Shouldn't

You Shouldn't

You Shouldn't

You Shouldn't

You Shouldn't

You Shouldn't

You Shouldn't

You Shouldn't

You Shouldn't

You Shouldn't

You Shouldn't

You Shouldn't

.

You Shouldn't

You Shouldn't

You Shouldn't

You Shouldn't

You Shouldn't

You Shouldn't

You Shouldn't

You Shouldn't

You Shouldn't

You Shouldn't

You Shouldn't

You Shouldn't

You Shouldn't

You Shouldn't

You Shouldn't

You Shouldn't

You Shouldn't

You Shouldn't

You Shouldn't

You Shouldn't

You Shouldn't

You Shouldn't

You Shouldn't

You Shouldn't

You Shouldn't

You Shouldn't

You Shouldn't

You Shouldn't

You Shouldn't

You Shouldn't

You Shouldn't

You Shouldn't

You Shouldn't

You Shouldn't

You Shouldn't

You Shouldn't

You Shouldn't

You Shouldn't

You Shouldn't

You Shouldn't

You Shouldn't

You Shouldn't

You Shouldn't

You Shouldn't

You Shouldn't

You Shouldn't

You Shouldn't

You Shouldn't

You Shouldn't

You Shouldn't

You Shouldn't

You Shouldn't

You Shouldn't

You Shouldn't

You Shouldn't

You Shouldn't

You Shouldn't

You Shouldn't

You Shouldn't

You Shouldn't

You Shouldn't

You Shouldn't

You Shouldn't

You Shouldn't

You Shouldn't

You Shouldn't

You Shouldn't

You Shouldn't

You Shouldn't

You Shouldn't

You Shouldn't

You Shouldn't

Printed in Poland
by Amazon Fulfillment
Poland Sp. z o.o., Wrocław

52526332R00119